Stepping Into The Now Anointing

Bennie Baker

Bennie Baker Ministries
Calvary Pentecostal Church International

Email: benniebakerMinistries@gmail.com
Website: www.benniebaker.com

Stepping Into The Now Anointing

By: Bennie D. Baker

Printed in the United States

Introduction

The stories and teaching you are about to read was birthed at a new level of faith that God called the Whole Baker Family to in 2016. All of us from my wife and I to our unborn grand baby who was born right smack dab in the middle of our transition. This was both the most exciting year of our life and at the same time, it was one of the hardest years of our lives. But through it all, God is always faithful. I am so thankful for my precious wife and children who walked right beside me the whole way. I am so thankful for the gift God has given me in my family. Many of you reading this book are going through your own battles. Maybe you are like me and in the biggest transitional season of your life, in your job, in your ministry, and/or in your family and you need God to move for you now. Well my friend, I want you to know that I believe that God is going to move for you NOW! The same faithful father that brought the Baker family through the toughest season of our lives will be faithful to bring you through as well.

It's My Time

Preciouses reader, I want you to say this out loud, **"It's my time!"** Go ahead shout it out loud, I want you to hear yourself saying it. **"It's My Time!"** Somebody is going to get set free today, so it might as well be you. Somebody is getting a breakthrough today, so it might as well be you! This is your time for a now miracle!

Miriam Webster say that the word **now** means; A*t this present time or in this moment.* Have you ever needed God to move now? You don't feel you have time to wait for all the things that well-meaning people have told you must wait for in order to get your breakthrough. When you have a son or daughter who needs to be saved, you need them saved in the now. When you get a bad report from the doctor, you don't have time to wait ten years. You need God to move now.

I don't want you to think I'm taking away from the power of waiting. Waiting is a powerful biblical principle that every believer should practice. What I propose to you, in this teaching, is there is an appropriate time to believe for the now! My challenge is for you to increase your faith! Be willing to believe for God to do something bigger than you have ever believed for in your life. Believe for Him to do faster than you ever believed for in your life. Believe for God to do something so big that the world will have to stand back and say only God could have done that. I heard a wise man say onetime,

> "Good things come to those who wait but they only get what those who hustle leave behind."

Such wise words right there. It's good to wait but let's not allow our waiting to become an excuse. You must let your faith soar and believe for the very best God has for you. It's time to not take no for an answer, but to go in and possess the land.

Desperation

There are two kinds of desperation I want to
share with you about. The first is the kind of
desperation that is birthed out of a need. There
is no better biblical reference to desperation
than 2 Kings 4. This precious daughter was
desperate for a miracle. First, her husband died.
She has more than likely just finished a time of
mourning. The Jewish people call this time of
mourning after the death of a loved one called,
"Shiva." This is seven days of discomfort they
put on themselves so they can reflect on the loss
they just suffered. Also, since this was the loss
of a husband, there was another ceremony she
participated in called, "Sit Shiva." This was a
time during the mourning process that called
for close family and friends to come to the Shiva
house and mourn together. Can you imagine the
emotional strain of losing a loved one then
spending seven days, 24 hours a day, with
family? As though having the family all in one
house 24 seven isn't stressful enough. And then
after going through this time of intense
mourning and just as the last mourner leaves,
the last piece of food was served, and this

broken women steps back to take a breath, there is a knock at the door.

> # Desperation Brings You To a place where you must believe for the now!

She rises from her chair, moves slowly to the door, wondering who could this be. As she opens the door, she sees a well-dressed business man with a stack of papers in his hands who greets her with a smile. She does not recognize the man but she does recognize the letter head on the papers in his hands. It was someone her husband had done business with years ago. Maybe he was there about some land her husband had owned that she did not know about. Was there possibility of a hidden blessing she was unaware of?

She reads the documents in disbelief because they said they were here to take her children to work off her husband's debt. She knew how these things worked and once they took her children the debt would never be paid. They would be lost in a system that they could never be able to get out of. This couldn't be! This was not happening! She slammed the door in the face of the debt collector. The man pounded on the door, the smile on his face is now gone and he shouts from outside, "By this time tomorrow, I'll have the money or I will be taking your children away."

Can you imagine after losing her husband, she is now faced with losing her children too? She needed God to move NOW! This is the kind of desperation that says if God does not move for me now, I'm finished. This child of God has a financial need that demands Gods attention now. What was she supposed to do? Try to refinance? There was no time for that! Get a loan from a family member? There was no time for that either! Restructure her business? NO!

There was no time for any of that! If God did not move for her she was finished.

This story tells the true tale of a daughter who was desperate because of her situation. Her lack brought her to a place of desperation. But you don't have to be driven to a place of desperation. You can you walk in a desperation for God and His purpose for your life. This kind of desperation will also cause you to step into your now anointing. When you are so desperate for God that you are willing to pray every day at 5:00 AM, willing to go without a bite of food for days, so desperate that you sow a significant seed, these things will put you in a position to receive a now anointing.

You may be saying, like the widow, "I don't have much here, I can't do as much as other people can do for the kingdom." Or some might say that they don't have any special gifts talents or abilities. Well my friend, I have good news! It does not matter if there are people out there that can out sing you, out pray you, out give you, out praise you or travel to nations that you may only hear about. All those things may be outside of your control. But you decide how desperate you are for the things of God. You set the gauge on how hungry you are and what you are willing to do to get your breakthrough!

Sowing For A Now Miracle

A few months ago, I received a phone call from a partner who needed God to move now. She told me a story of how her husband had gone through a difficult financial time years before they were married and there was a substantial tax bill that never got paid. It wasn't long until the collection calls began. They had tried for years to settle the debt with no progress. In fact, the situation didn't get better it got worse. This debt had now snow-balled into an $80,000 debt. In desperation, she called me and told me about the situation and sowed a substantial seed. You might say that makes no sense. She had a debt and she was going to give money away? My friend, we must move outside the systems of the world and put our trust in the kingdom of God. We will never see the miraculous until we are willing to sow the ridiculous. I agreed with her over the phone for a now miracle. After we hung up, I added her to our prayer list and Pastor Judah and I began praying for her every day.

It was just a few days later this dear partner called me back. She said she just opened a letter from the bill collector that said the account was settled in full and they had enclosed a check for $300.00. Oh, come on somebody! She entered into a now anointing. She did not have time to settle. She did not have time wait. She needed God to move now. Friend, God is no respecter of persons. If He can do it for her, He can do it for you.

It was 2001 and I was pastoring in Waterloo, Iowa. I was so desperate for a move of God, praying hours every day, believing every minute for a breakthrough. We had come to a troubled church. There were very few people and no finances, but we had a word from God. The Lord told me to go, so we went. When we took the church, we lived in the basement of the church for the first six months. There were no living quarters. It was me, my wife and our three children, held up in a children's class room and a youth room. These were not ideal accommodations, but it was what was necessary for us to do what God had called us to do for a season.

When we took the church, there was a mortgage and another $70,000 debt the church owed that was there when we came. We believed we would have the time necessary to take care of this after the church had grown and got back on its feet. June of 2001 was the first of many great revivals we experienced in our time there. The church had grown numerically and was just getting together financially. My family and I were preparing to move into a small apartment when we received a call from the group the money was owed to. They said they wanted the money and they wanted it right away. We explained the situation to them and asked if we could work this out over time. This plea fell on deaf ears and they told us if we could not repay the debt, they were taking the church building from us. We were still living in the church at that time and it looked like we were going to be homeless, churchless, jobless and out on the streets in a matter of days if God did not move now! Over the next few days we prayed, fasted, and sought God desperately for a word. We were desperate for a breakthrough! We were desperate for God to move now! A few days later, I found myself at a minister's conference, desperate for God to speak a word to me and to give me some form of direction. At the end of the service, I was called out and given a word by my Apostle, Bobby Hogan, who told me," You're in the biggest battle of your life, but you are about to have the greatest victory of your life." Now I had a word.

"Your Greatest Battles Lead to Your Greatest Victories"

A few days later, our debt was called. The people showed up at the church and told us if we didn't settle this debt now, they were throwing us out and taking the building. To some, this might look like a grim situation, but I had received a NOW word. By the grace of God and the Power of Holy Spirit, we had slipped into a NOW season. The word I got was, "I may be in a battle but I'm going to have the victory." And I was going to stand on that word. We still didn't have money, but we had a word. We were told we needed to evacuate the premises immediately and they left the property.

You may not have the money, but you can have the faith

Now within just a few minutes, these same people drove around the block and pulled right back into the church's parking lot. We watched from the front door of the church, as the same man walked up to the door shaking his head. He walked in still shaking his head and said," I don't know why I'm doing this, but I am forgiving your debt." They said that we did not owe them a dime and that they would draw up the papers the next day. Within 24 hours the papers were signed and we took full possession of our church! Just like that, we had stepped into our NOW anointing! This was such a major victory in our lives and one of many we have seen God perform, but I believe the best is yet to come!

Immediately

God wants to move now for His children. There are so many now moments that fill the pages of the Bible. St. John 6 tells us the story of Jesus walking on the water. Jesus had just fed the five thousand and had slipped away for a little while. The disciples went down to the shore to wait for Jesus. In John's telling of this story, Jesus was not there and the disciples had waited a long time. They must have had some dead line that we don't know about or maybe they were tired of waiting, but for some reason they got in the boat and made their way to the other side. Not long after getting into the boat, a great wind begin to blow in out of nowhere and the boat began to rock back and forth. "What a storm," the disciples must have thought. "I haven't seen a storm like this since that time Jesus was asleep in the bottom of the boat." Then their whole attitude changed as they realized the severity of the storm they were in. After rowing for hours and hours only going a short distance, they must have thought they were never going to get to the other side. Friend, have you been there? You feel like you have done everything God has required of you. You have stood, prayed, fasted, been faithful when no one else had, but it seemed like you were no closer to your breakthrough than when you started. If that's you, go ahead and throw your party now! Because you are a prime candidate to fall into the "Now Anointing!"

The Bible is unclear as to when Jesus decided to step out onto the water and cross over to the other side of the sea, but Mark's gospel says

Jesus had no intentions of getting in the disciple's boat.

> *Mark 6:48 And he saw them toiling in rowing; for the wind was contrary unto them: and about the fourth watch of the night he cometh unto them, walking upon the sea, and would have passed by them.*

Jesus would have passed them by, but He saw them struggling. Loved one, Jesus sees you when you're struggling! If you're not struggling today, then when you have struggled in your past or when you will struggle in your future, Jesus will see you. Your struggle is an opportunity for Jesus to jump into your life and give you your NOW breakthrough. So, Jesus reroutes His trip, gets into their boat and then something powerful happens.

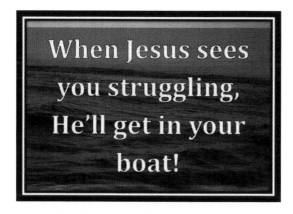

*St. John 6:21 Then they willingly received him into the ship: and **immediately** the ship was at the land whither they went.*

When Jesus got in the boat, they were immediately at their destination. Hallelujah! These experienced fishermen who knew the sea well, were in a storm so bad that they got turned around and did not know where they were or if they could make it to shore. But they went from the middle of a storm in the middle of the lake, to where they were supposed to be in the blink of an eye! This all happen because Jesus got in their boat! They just stepped into a "Now Anointing!" Someone reading this book right now is stepping into their NOW anointing!

If you have been in a storm of some kind, then get ready to step into this "Now Anointing!" I want to release a word to you, the reader of this book, that will propel you into a place of faith. A word that will cause you to see yourself walking on the water with Jesus into the breakthrough that God the Father says you can have. To do that, God has given me a few steps for you that I believe will charge your faith and push you into your NOW anointing.

1. Believe For Your Breakthrough

Have faith to believe for your breakthrough. Sounds so easy, doesn't it? Having faith is not hard, but when you are staring down an unpaid bill or a budget that's not met or a physical problem that has you riddled with pain, it can seem easier said than done. But loved one, you can have your breakthrough despite your current situation. It is when these things come into our lives that we can believe, no matter what it looks like. I have heard people say, "What if I believe for it and nothing happens?" Our heavenly Father doesn't want His children operating in doubt of any kind. He has everything you'll ever need. So, what if it does happen?! What if you believe for God to move NOW and you get exactly what you believe for?

> *Matthew 21:22 And all things, whatsoever ye shall ask in prayer, believing, ye shall receive.*

Where is the "What if it doesn't happen?" in this scripture? Matthew tells us that if we pray and if we believe, then we will receive. It really is that simple.

We eat a lot of rice in our house. Rice is one of my favorite things to eat. I love fried rice, chicken and rice, and plain brown rice...and if the next day, we have some left-over rice, I love to eat that rice with milk, sugar and a little cinnamon. Rice is a versatile meal and often seems to be in an abundance in our house. Rice has great nutritional value. In fact, when we eat rice, we eat brown rice. I read somewhere that white rice is only brown rice that they have processed and what they took from the rice, not only made it white but, is used to make medicine. The only problem I have with rice is, that sometimes when I eat some sort of rice dish, I'm hungry again two hours later. So even though I feel a certain way after I have eaten rice, I must trust the fact that what's inside that rice is exactly what I need to survive. Just because I got hungry again after I ate rice, doesn't mean I give up on rice forever. The same is true after eating a big steak dinner. You will get hungry again. You must trust that, in your steak dinner, was everything you needed to survive. I have no plans on giving up on steak dinners! The same is true with believing. If you did not get the result you hoped for, believe again and again and again. You must trust that, while you are believing, God is doing exactly what you are believing for even if you don't feel it or see it. There is nothing that is impossible for God.

> Romans 8:38 For I am persuaded, that neither death, nor life, nor angels, nor principalities, nor powers, nor things present, nor things to come, 39 Nor height, nor depth, nor any other creature, shall be able to separate us from the love of God, which is in Christ Jesus our Lord.

Paul is telling us not to allow the world around us to shape what we believe. Our feelings, past experiences, or what we see going on right now, none of these things have power over God's plan for our lives. God wants His word to shape our future and shape our present. Coming into 2017, God gave me a word, "Watch your words." Your future will be shaped by your words. Provers 18:21 tells us that the power of life and death are in the tongue. You have, in your possession, the power to speak life over every future and present situation in your life. As you begin to speak words of faith over your family, over your job, over your ministry, or over your life, you will see the power of the words you speak come alive! And you will be *who* you say you are. This is also true if you speak death. So friend, choose your words wisely...speak life!

Don't be afraid to ask God for a NOW breakthrough.

Many times, believers think it's wrong to ask God to do something now. This is a misconception sent from the enemy. God wants you to believe for now things. It takes faith to believe for now and God wants His children to walk in faith.

Luke 18:27 And he said, the things which are impossible with men are possible with God.

After sharing this revelation on the "Now anointing" last year in Des Moines, Iowa, a dear sister came to one of my services and requested prayer for her son. He was in the military and had been missing for over a month. She was overcome with tears, crying out. She said she just needed to know that he was ok. She did not know if he was. If he was sick, lost, injured or worse, she did not know. She needed the peace that comes with knowing all is well with her child. We prayed fervently with her, asking the Lord to move every obstacle in the way and let her know her son was safe, NOW. The next day, as I was on my way to Texas for another revival, this dear lady with the missing son contacted me. She said within a few hours after we prayed, her son called her and let her know he was fine! Hallelujah! She stepped into the NOW anointing.

2. Have Faith For Big Things

Jeremiah 32:17 Ah Lord GOD! behold, thou hast made the heaven and the earth by thy great power and stretched out arm, and there is nothing too hard for thee:

Wow! We serve such a big God! We serve a God who has made heaven and earth with His own hand. There is nothing that ever was, is or will be that God's own fingerprint is not on. Jeremiah also reminds us of this powerful truth, "There is nothing too hard for God." The Lord is telling His children that it's ok to dream big! May you have a small business in a small town and there has not been much growth over the past few years and you have said to yourself this is just how it is. It's just a small town or a small market and that's just how it is. That's just the kind of lie the enemy wants you to believe. But there is nothing is too hard for God! He can draw business from other towns or He can cause your business to explode online or he can bring in one client or customer that can bring more blessing in one year than all your other years combined. Just dream big!

Joseph was a big dreamer and in his youth, he dreamed of how all his family would bow to him. But that dream seemed more like a nightmare when he was thrown into a pit by the people who were supposed to bow to him. But this did not kill his dream. When he was sold into slavery by his own family, it did not kill his dream. When he was a slave in a pagan's house, it did not kill his dream. When he was wrongfully accused and thrown into prison, that still did not kill his dream. But when his dream caught up with his reality, God challenged Joseph to dream even bigger. Not only did his family bow to him, but a whole nation bowed to him!

God is not slack in moving big for His children! Since you are one of His, then He will not be slack in moving big for you. So go ahead and ask Him for something big.

3. Talk The Talk, & Walk The Walk

The next few pages are very important, so read carefully. It is very difficult to believe God for big things like a new house when you have never believed God for a house payment. Unfortunately, there are always those that will say they're believing God for a million-dollar mansion, but have never believed God for anything else. What they are doing is almost mocking God because they have no intention of ever getting a million-dollar home. They just think is sounds spiritual. There is a very heavy price for such behavior because many times, these people's family and children end up having a hard time walking in faith later. They have a hard time because they have never seen the fruit of what their parents or loved ones were believing for. So, to avoid having the responsibility of fully walking by faith, some will shoot for the moon with no intention of ever hitting it. I know this may be a heavy truth for some, but be aware of the accountability that comes with saying I am believing God for something. These should never be idle words. Jesus talks about these kind people in Matthew.

> *Matthew 15:18 This people draweth nigh unto me with their mouth, and honoureth me with their lips; but their heart is far from me.*

But rest assured my friends, if you are in the word, praying and standing on that word, and believing every day without doubting, you are going to get your breakthrough! And when you come to the realization that God wants the very best He has for you no matter how big, that's when you start stepping into this NOW anointing.

4. Follow Instructions

Deuteronomy 29:9
Keep therefore the words of this covenant, and do them, that ye may prosper in all that ye do.

This is a such an important life application if you want to walk in the NOW anointing. All throughout Gods word, our Heavenly Father gives His children instructions on how to have everything His word says we can have. If you want the windows of heaven to open over you and your family, then follow the instructions given to you in Malachi;

Malachi 3:10 Bring ye all the tithes into the storehouse, that there may be meat in mine house, and prove me now herewith, saith the Lord of hosts, if I will not open you the windows of heaven, and pour you out a blessing, that there shall not be room enough to receive it.

If you want to be blessed, follow these instructions in Luke;

Luke 6:38; Give, and it shall be given unto you; good measure, pressed down, and shaken together, and running over, shall men give into your bosom. For with the same measure that ye mete withal it shall be measured to you again.

If you want to live a long life, follow these instructions given to us in Exodus;

Exodus 20:12 Honor thy father and thy mother: that thy days may be long upon the land which the LORD thy God giveth thee.

When the widow woman from 2 Kings 4 went to the prophet, she was given a set of instructions. Go and borrow empty vessels from your neighbors. Could you imagine the disaster if the vessels she borrowed would have been partially filled with something? That would

have impeded her ability to get the right price to be able to pay off all her debt. Elisha said, "Borrow not a few." What if she would have only borrowed a few. Once again, it would not have been enough to pay the debt. Go in and shut the door. These are very specific instructions. This isn't the only place God has given His people instructions. Divine instructions are all throughout the Bible. God told Moses to talk to a stone one time and strike it another. Moses' ability to follow God's instructions was a deciding factor in him entering or not entering the promise land.
You may be asking God for some big things. If so, then take the time to ask God for some instructions. He may speak them to you. He may direct you to someone who has a word for you. Or He may show you in a book or in the life of another believer. Seek out the instructions and the be faithful to follow them. Because God has good gifts that He is just waiting to give to you.

It is my prayer that through the words of this book, you see that God is not only capable of moving NOW, but He wants to.

God Has Good Gifts For You

Matthew 7:11 If ye then, being evil, know how to give good gifts unto your children, how much more shall your Father which is in heaven give good things to them that ask him?

As a father, I can really relate to this scripture. Anyone close to me knows that I am crazy about Christmas. Christmas is my favorite time of the year. The music, the lights, the TV specials, the message of Jesus being born, the presents, just all of it! I get so excited about Christmas day that I can't even sleep the night before. As I look back on Christmas as a child, it seemed so much about what was going to be under the tree with my name on it. I had a bunch of old radio programs from the golden age of radio on cassette. I used to listen to them every day and my favorite radio program was the "Lone Ranger." I would listen in amazement as the bandits would rob the train and the Lone Ranger, with the help of his faithful sidekick Tonto, would save the day. One Christmas, I asked for a Lone Ranger action figure. I'd lay awake at night thinking about the adventures I'd have with the Lone Ranger and Tonto at my side. I was a kid in the eighties and those were some of the best days of my life.

Today, Christmas is even more exciting to me than it was when I was a kid. Now I have a wife and three beautiful children. And in October of 2015, our first grand baby was born. Now Christmas is more exciting than it has ever been. There is nothing I enjoy more than getting Christmas gifts for my family. The look on my boys' face when they got their first bicycles, the look in my daughter's eye when she got her first Barbie doll, how my wife's eye light up when she got her first present from Tiffany's in a Tiffany's box, and the look on my grandbabies face when she climbs on her first power wheel, those are some of the greatest memories of my life.

But as much as I love to give, my heavenly Father loves to give so much more than I ever will. He gives in a way that I'll never be able to understand. Jesus tells us in Matthew 7, that if I want to give good gifts to my children, how much more does our heavenly Father want to give to us, His children. Our heavenly Father wants to move more for us than we even want Him to move ourselves. God wants to move NOW for us. It's not His plan for His children to struggle.

Now in this lifetime

Before we bring this book to a close I want to share with you how I received this NOW anointing. Many of you know that in the fall of 2015, my family and I made the largest transition of our lives. The Lord spoke to our hearts sometime back about leaving the church we had pastored for almost 15 years. When this first got in my spirit, it was a bit too much for me. I just did not know how it would all work out. When we came to Waterloo, Iowa in 2001, the church had been through such a difficult time. There were only a handful of people, no finances, no salary, or no place to live. We just went in faith. When we left Iowa, we left a strong foundation, there was a good salary for the next pastor, and a nice home. Through a miracle, we purchased a nice parsonage that we had personally done so much work on ourselves and we had made it our home. This was also the place our children grew up. So I asked the Lord, "How do I leave a church and people I love with all my heart and a community I was known, respected and loved in to go to a new place where there are no guarantees, no family, and no history. Also, I would be leaving behind my oldest son and his wife, who, at the time just happen to be pregnant with our first grand baby. I was both excited and scared at the same time. When I talked to my wife about the move, she was on board, our children were all on board, and I believed that God had spoken to my heart so He would work it all out.

I won't even try to explain to you what we went through our first few months in our new place. I have lived by faith for more than 20 years of my life, but I was in new territory now. I felt like a round peg in a square hole. But most of all, I missed my son who was not able to move with us. He had been married almost a year, with a baby on the way, a house, and a job. He was building a life in Iowa. Even though he understood his mom and dad were following God, he had to live the life God called him to live and I also understood he was providing for his family. But that did not take away the pain I felt every single day I was away from him. I grew up without a father. Being a dad is so important to me and being away from my son was just breaking my heart. But I had a word. The Lord had spoken to my heart and told me if we made this move, my whole family would be together. I did not know how this would work out, but I trusted the Lord and was willing to do what He told me to do. I was willing to wait as long as it took to reap the harvest God had for me. What my wife and I went through during this time, I would never want any person to ever go through. I never want to go through again, but I can stand and say, "God, I have not withheld anything from you."

> **For us to realize our destiny, sometimes God must move us to a place that is conducive for what he has for us to move through us.**

It was during this time that this scripture became more real to me than any other time in my life. Even though I had read it many times and preached and heard countless messages from it, in this season and for the first time, this verse came alive to me.

> *Mark 10:29And Jesus answered and said, Verily I say unto you, There is no man that hath left house, or brethren, or sisters, or father, or mother, or wife, or children, or lands, for my sake, and the gospel's, 30But he shall receive an hundredfold now in this time, houses, and brethren, and sisters, and*

mothers, and children, and lands, with persecutions; and in the world to come eternal life.

Jesus said "no man". What that means is, no one that has left house, brother, sister, father, mother, wife, or children. I want to stop there because Jesus said children. Now, Jesus has my attention because I have not withheld anything from him. When we relocated, we left a home we had built, we left family and friends we loved and I needed a harvest. Now that brings me to the next part of this scripture that got my attention. Jesus says, "**now in this lifetime.**" That means now, right now. At this present time or in this moment! If you have sowed good seed into the kingdom of God or if you have made sacrifices based on what God has told you to do, then you have the right to lay claim to the word NOW. That's what I did. I reminded God that I had sowed.

Not long after I preached this message for the first time, I was driving down the road on a Sunday morning to minister at a church in Northwest Arkansas. I got a call from my son who tells me there has been a series of events that have taken place in his life. He has talked it over with his wife and he wanted to let me know that they were moving to Arkansas to be with us. Now I have seen God bring millions of dollars into the kingdom. I have seen people get up out of wheel chairs. I've seen brain cancer healed, broken bones mended and many more miracles than I can even remember. But when I heard the words, "Dad, we are moving to where you are," this was the biggest miracle of my life! Not because it was the hardest, but it was the biggest desire of my heart! God moved for me and He did it in the NOW! I could not begin to tell you about all the shouting, praising, and testifying that went on over this awesome miracle God gave us now. Friend, what God did for Pastors Judah and Bennie Baker, He can do for you. He is no respecter of persons and what He did for us, He'll do for you.

Thank you so much for giving us the opportunity to share this powerful revelation with you. I believe your faith has been ignited and you are going to see God move big for you NOW! There are so many NOW miracles, I can't wait to share with you including one about our new home. So keep us in your prayers as we are praying for you and remember your best is yet to come!

Sow A Seed

Each month we ask our friends and partners to sow a $30.00 seed of favor into our outreach ministry. I pray you would consider that seed and consider partnering with us. Help us spread the love of Jesus all over the world. If you would like to sow a seed or to find more of our ministry resources, go to www.benniebaker.com. While you're there, be sure to sign up for our email newsletter, follow us on Facebook, Twitter, and Instagram. Thank you again for your investment into the kingdom of God.

Other Resources Available

Uncommon – CD $	12.00
David's Fight – CD	12.00
It's in The Bag – CD	12.00
Pieces – CD	12.00
Let Him Dance – CD	12.00
Sons and Servants – CD	12.00
Favor – CD	12.00
Process to Promo.. – CD	12.00
The Blood – CD	12.00
The Ravens Are Coming – CD	12.00
Lord of The Storm – CD	12.00
Don't Let the Limp Fool You – CD	12.00
Jesus Brought the Fire – CD	12.00
Shipwreck Faith – CD	12.00
Spirit of The Elder Brother – CD	12.00
God Will Remember You – CD	12.00
Fire On the Mountain – CD	12.00
Freedom Riders – CD	12.00

- - - - - - - - - -

Spirit of the Elder Brother – Book	12.00
There Ain't No Shame In That – Book	12.00
Miracles at the Door – Book	12.00

(Postage and handling included)
To order one of these life changing products
Call 319-895-2329 www.benniebaker.com
Mail Check or Money Order to P.O. Box 1482 Van Buren, AR

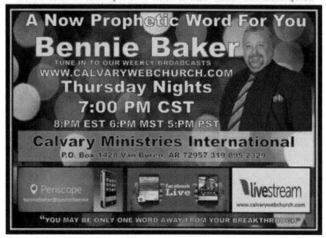

Made in the USA
Middletown, DE
12 June 2022

67016746R00022